The Left-Right Reversal Screening Tool

Quickly and Easily Screen Your Student for Letter and Number Reversals

by Bridgette O'Neill

Contents

What are Letter Reversals?

Reversing letters means your child reads and writes certain letters (or numbers) backwards or upside down. In writing, this can be referred to as mirror writing. Your child may write a b when it needs a d. But this can also happen when reading; words like dog end up being read as bog, etc.

Word reversals can also happen, words like *saw* and *was* get confused in both reading and writing.

Transposing letters is different. When letters are transposed in a word, it means switching the order of letters, such as *bread* being written or read as *beard* or vise versa.

The most common letter reversal is *b* and *d*, when the child reads or writes a *b* for a *d* or vice versa. Another common reversal is *p* and *q*. It's also possible that children write some letters backwards like *k* and *j*, having the tail or arms of the letter facing the wrong direction.

An example of an upside-down reversal is *m* for *w*.

The most common number reversal is *6*. It can be mistaken as a 9, or just written completely backwards, resembling a 2 when handwritten. However, most of the numbers can be written backwards.

Are Reversals a Sign of Dyslexia?

One of the most common concerns of many parents is that their child reverses their letters, numbers and words. Parents have a real fear that if their child reverses letters or other symbols, he or she is dyslexic or has a learning disability. This is not always the case.

It's normal and expected that most young children will reverse letters or words.

The distinction appears with the frequency, the age of the child, and the extent at which the child reverses letters.

In *Developing Ocular Motor and Visual Perception Skills*, Kenneth Lane describes the following regarding expectations with reversals:

"Children need a mental age of 5 ½ to 6 ½ to overcome 'up-down' (vertical) reversals and 7 ½ for 'left-right' (horizontal) reversals (Harman, 1982). By the end of second grade, reversals occur only among the poorest readers (Fischer, 1971). By the age of 9 or 10 years, children are said to code spatial location in adult-like fashion, enabling them to understand how the relationships among objects would appear at various angles (Wallace, 2001)."

Number reversals, such as 6 and 9 and 5 and 2, commonly occur up to about ages five and six, and the reversals of letters b and d and p and q should be corrected by age 7 1/2. Older elementary children should grasp the concept of directionality and no longer demonstrate problems with reversals.

If reversals are numerous or continue into second and third grade or beyond, then remedial measures may need to be looked at.

Do Kids Outgrow Reversing Letters?

It's not uncommon or unusual to see young children of 4, 5 and 6 years of age making letter, number or word reversals.

The majority of kids will outgrow reversals as they age and improve their reading, writing, working memory and visual perception skills. Reversals are typical and fairly common through first grade.

That's because the letters *b*, *d*, *p*, and *q* are really all the same letter. They're just flipped and turned, or oriented differently. Experienced readers have learned that letter orientation makes a big difference.

Young kids and beginning readers don't always make that distinction right away, though. That discovery is part of the learning process. It comes as kids build their visual processing skills and become more experienced readers and writers.

If your child is still reversing a lot of letters by the end of first grade, you may want to look into mediation techniques.

Letter Reversals – What's Normal?

Young children often bring home schoolwork that has letter, number and word reversals on it. While they are young, it seems to be age appropriate, but if the problem continues into second and third grade, parents should be concerned.

It's important to first understand what to expect with reversals according to the mental age of the child. The mental age of your child is the concept of how their age relates to the average intellectual performance of other children at the same age. Mental age can be slightly different than the physical age of your child.

Norm referenced tests show that it is completely normal, or average, for five year old boys to make 5 reversals on a test of 68 items, or a 7% error rate.

However, girls of the same age should score slightly higher, having an average error rate of 4 or less out of 68 items, or a 6% error rate.

For your convenience, a norm reference table is included in the *Grading the Assessment* section of this book.

Types of Reversals : Static Reversals

There are two different types of reversals that a child can struggle with when they struggle with reversals. The first type is *static reversals* and the second is *kinetic reversals.* There are distinct differences with each type.

Static reversals happen when the child is confused on the proper orientation of the letter, or the directionality of the letter, such as writing a *b* as a *d*, a *p* as a *q* or writing the tail of *j* in the wrong direction.

Young children are literal and concrete thinkers. If they see a chair, it's a chair no matter what position it's in. If a chair faces right, it's still a chair. If it faces left, it's still a chair. If the chair is upside down, it's still a chair. This is a 3-D spatial understanding.

However, letters, numbers and words are all symbols. They're 2-D representations of concepts. The letter b represents the phonological sound /b/. When a b is forward facing, it represents the sound /b/, but when the symbol is reversed, d, it represents the sound /d/. If you take the exact same symbol and flip it upside down facing forward, p, it represents the sound /p/ and when it is upside down and backward facing, q, it represents the sound /q/. The exact same symbol represents four different sounds. The only difference between them is how the symbol is oriented.

It's easy to understand how young children would confuse them.

That's why the solution for reversals contains several factors: working memory, visual spatial skills, visual tracking skills and even neuromotor skills when writing the letters, numbers and words.

Types of Reversals : Kinetic Reversals

Kinetic reversals occur when a child is creating the pencil strokes on paper, showing a tendency to confuse words that are mirror images of each other such as *saw* and *was, ton* and *not*. This is a neuromotor issue with the hand motions of the child.

All letters do not begin at the same starting point or move in the same direction. This can be a problem for young students. Their hands actually learn the movements in one way and then try to make other letters fit that movement. So a student may begin writing the letter b at the top and move down into a bubble. The normal verbal cue for b is "long line down, bounce around." But some students will try to write a d following the same directions, only bouncing in the other direction. This will increase b/d confusion.

That's why it's imperative that handwriting is taught with proper visual and verbal cues and in a very explicit order, grouping letters that are written in the same way together. If students learn to write their letters in this systematic way, they will avoid many reversal issues.

Visual Processing Issues

If a child struggles past the age of seven with reversals, they may have a visual processing issue, or more specifically a visual discrimination problem. The child can't identify and compare features of symbols, like letters, numbers, or words.

Sometimes, a visual discrimination issue goes along with other learning disabilities. Dyslexia is the most common learning disability with writing and reading issues, and reversals are typically part of it. However, much of the time, this is not the case.

Many students can exhibit issues with visual processing. A good reversal remediation program will include visual processing exercises and visual tracking exercises to strengthen these skills.

How Can I Help My Child At Home?

There was a time when training and materials weren't available to parents. Students had to rely on well trained teachers or attend years of therapy with a speech therapist. This is no longer the case.

As more studies are published showing what exact deficits lead to reversals, materials are being made to remedy the problems.

Steps you can take at home:

•   Follow an explicit method for teaching handwriting. Letters are grouped by their starting position and orientation. Problematic letters are separated and written in different ways. Each letter is taught with specific visual and verbal cues, therefore utilizing all three main learning pathways; visual, auditory and kinesthetic.

•   Strengthen your student's working memory skills with working memory games using problematic letters.

•   Strengthen your student's visual processing and visual tracking skills.

•   Do hemispheric integration exercises, or brain balancing exercises with your student.

•   Give your student ample practice with letter and word reading and dictation.

You can purchase specialized workbooks in each of these areas or you can purchase one highly effective program that includes all of the above mentioned techniques.

Flipping Letters: Techniques to Eliminate Letter and Number Reversals by Bridgette O'Neill was created to help parents, teachers and tutors eliminate letter and number reversals with their students.

Flipping Letters: What's in Each Lesson?

1. Multisensory Handwriting Intervention

Letters and numbers are taught using specific visual and verbal cues. This intervention targets *visual learners, auditory learners and kinesthetic learners*. It also builds *motor memory* making reversals less common.

2. Build Memory

In this activity students review the model letter, the visual cues and the verbal cues, then they write the letter from memory. This is one of the only research based methods proven to reduce reversals *substantially*.

3. Visual Tracking Exercises

In this multi sensory activity, students scan for the target letter. This builds visual tracking skills, scanning skills, attention to detail and focus while reinforcing letter *automaticity*.

4. Brain Balancing Exercises

Targeted letters are used in hemispheric integration exercises to reinforce letter *automaticity* while building neural networks to support learning.

5. Word Reading and Dictation

Students practice mastery of the target letter by reading a list of words and then a sentence, with and without distractors. The list and sentence are then dictated for the student to write.

BONUS Memory Game with EVERY Lesson

Build visual letter memory and auditory letter memory with this fun little game. It only takes 2 minutes! Build letter recognition and orientation automaticity with this quick and easy game.

BONUS Activities

Extra letter mazes are included throughout as well as bonus review sections to assist students in mastery of each letter.

The Left-Right Reversal Screening Tool

The Left-Right Reversal Screening Tool is an assessment that you can give your student at home. It takes about five minutes to give the assessment and about 10 – 15 minutes to grade it.

With the assessment, you can quickly gauge where your student stands in regards to reversing letters and numbers. Are they average, above average or below average? How do they compare with other students their age? Do you need a remediation program?

This screening tool is not an affirmative test and should not be given as such. It's used to screen students for the purpose of tracking their progress.

You should give the assessment to your student, grade it and then follow a remediation program. When your student completes the remediation program, give the assessment again and gauge their progress.

Giving the Assessment

1.   Prepare a quiet place for your student to take the assessment. There should be no distractions; tv, radio, computer, phone or other children, present. All distractions should be eliminated.

2.   Place your child where they cannot see written words, letters or numbers. I.e. Do not place your child in a room facing a clock or picture with writing on it.

3.   Give your child the student form (several copies are included in this book)

4.   Instruct your child to look carefully at each letter and number. If the letter or number is right, then leave it alone. Instruct them to circle any letter or number that 'looks wrong'. DO NOT give them explicit directions to look for backwards or reversed letters. If they ask any questions, just repeat the directions. Do not over-explain the exercise.

5.   Leave the child alone to complete the assessment. Standing over the child may make them nervous. If you watch them take the assessment and make sounds or motions when they answer incorrectly, your child may be able to read your signals and the test results won't be accurate.

6.   Once your student has completed the assessment, grade it in another room without your student present. DO NOT grade the assessment in front of your student.

Grading the Assessment

1. Grade the assessment at a time and place where your student will not be present. Students are often already very sensitive to their own weaknesses and may feel like a poor score on the assessment 'proves' that something is wrong with them. We do not want to feed into that idea.

2. Compare the completed student form with the included Answer Key. There are 26 reversed letters and numbers on the answer key.

3. If your student circled a correctly oriented letter or number, mark it wrong, such as the lowercase b or d. Cross the incorrect answers out.

4. If your student did not circle a reversed letter or number, mark that wrong, such as the reversed 6. Cross out incorrect answers.

5. Count how many crossed out (incorrect) answers are on the student form. This is their 'Error Count'.

6. Compare your student's error count with the Norms and Developmental Age.

Grading the Assessment: Norms

BOYS

Boys aged 5 years old: Less than 5 errors is Above Average
Boys aged 5 years old: 5 errors is Average
Boys aged 5 years old: More than 5 errors is Below Average

Boys aged 6 years old: Less than 4 errors is Above Average
Boys aged 6 years old: 4 errors is Average
Boys aged 6 years old: More than 4 errors is Below Average

Boys aged 7 years old: Less than 3 errors is Above Average
Boys aged 7 years old: 3 errors is Average
Boys aged 7 years old: More than 3 errors is Below Average

Boys aged 8+ years old: Less than 2 errors is Above Average
Boys aged 8+ years old: 2 errors is Average
Boys aged 8+ years old: More than 2 errors is Below Average

GIRLS

Girls aged 5 years old: Less than 4 errors is Above Average
Girls aged 5 years old: 4 errors is Average
Girls aged 5 years old: More than 4 errors is Below Average

Girls aged 6 years old: Less than 3 errors is Above Average
Girls aged 6 years old: 3 errors is Average
Girls aged 6 years old: More than 3 errors is Below Average

Girls aged 7 years old: Less than 2 errors is Above Average
Girls aged 7 years old: 2-3 errors is Average
Girls aged 7 years old: More than 2-3 errors is Below Average

Girls aged 8+ years old: Less than 2 errors is Above Average
Girls aged 8+ years old: 2 errors is Average
Girls aged 8+ years old: More than 2 errors is Below Average

Grading the Assessment: Developmental Age

In order to read your student's developmental age:

1. Find how many errors they had on the assessment
2. In the boys or girls column, find the age (years.months)of average students of that gender with the same number of errors.
3. For example: If the student is a 6 year old boy who made 3 errors; he scored in the normal range and has a developmental age of 6 years and 6 months old.
4. If the student is an 8 year old girl with 4 errors; she scored below average with a developmental age of 5 years old.
5. If the student is a 5 year old boy with 2 errors; he scored above average with a developmental age of 7 years and 6 months old.

ERRORS	BOYS	GIRLS
0	9.0+	9.0+
1	8.6	8.6
2	7.6	7.0
3	6.6	5.6
4	5.6	5.0
5	5.0	<5.0
6	<5.0	

STUDENT FORM

RTILCWDGQ

NAAPMSHBL

VKXZUJEOF

x r e s k d c t z

m i d l o f n u b

c r s a n h e t l

7 3 2 5 9 6 0

4 7 3 1 6 5

RTILCWDGQ

NAAPMSHBI

VKXZULEOF

x r e z k d c t z

d u n t o f u b   m i q j p i m

c r e a n h e t l

7 3 2 5 9 6 0

4 7 3 l 6 5

RTLCWDGQ
NAAPMSHBL
VKXZUJEOF

x r e s k d c t z
m j q l o t n u b
c r s a n h e t l

7 3 2 5 9 6 0
4 7 3 l 6 3 5

RTILCWDGQ

NEAPMSHBL

VKXZUJEOF

xreskdotz

miqjofnub

crzanhetl

7825960

4731635

QDGWCLITR
NAAPMSHBL
VKXZULEOF

xrɘꙅꞰbɔƚꙅ
nuꟼoⅎjbim
ɔꞮɘɒnɒʜɘⅎl

7Ɛ253ᖾ60
ᖾ7Ɛ1ᖾ3ᖋ

Q G D W C L T R

N A A P M S H B L

V K X Z U L E O F

z t d c k s e r x

d u n t o f j p i m

c r e a n h e t l

7 3 2 5 9 6 0

5 6 1 3 7 4

What Do I Do Now?

We recommend the complete reversals program in "Flipping Letters: Techniques to Eliminate Letter and Number Reversals" which teaches each of the steps outlined in this book along with techniques and tips. It can be found here www.ADHDReading.com

Simply print out and use each lesson in sequence. Your student can do one lesson a day.

You can also purchase a paperback copy from Amazon here: https://amzn.to/396G1Y8

The program is designed for **one-on-one intervention**. Print out the lesson pages, read the given directions to your student and then observe and correct as needed. Each daily lesson should take no more than 30 minutes.

This method of distributed practice and spaced repetition has been used to support effective learning for over 100 years.

Each lesson includes everything you need to target reversals:

- **Handwriting Techniques** with Specific **Visual Cues** for Visual Learners

- **Verbal Cues** for Auditory Learners

- **Motor Memory** activities for Kinesthetic Learners

- A Specialized **Memory Building** Intervention

- A **Visual Working Memory** Game

- **Visual Tracking** Exercises

- **Brain Balancing** Exercises

- Word **Reading** and **Dictation**

Students repeat lessons until they master each letter with fewer reversal occurrences.

For stubborn reversals complete one lesson (in example: *All About b*) every day for one week and then review a week later when introducing the new lesson. Some review is built into the lessons.

flipping letters

techniques to eliminate letter reversals

the most comprehensive program to
eliminate letter and number reversals

pairing research proven methods with a
step-by-step easy to follow program

bridgette o'neill

More Educational Workbooks from Gifted Brain Studios

Flipping Letters: Techniques to Eliminate Letter and Number Reversals
https://www.adhdreading.com/product-page/flipping-letters-reversal-workbook

Visual Tracking Sight Words: Visual Tracking Exercises with 100 High Frequency Sight Words https://amzn.to/31KmLfx

Brain Training Exercises to Boost Brain Power: for Improved Memory, Focus and Cognitive Function https://amzn.to/2Zc2ga6

Visual Tracking Exercises: Visual Perception, Visual Discrimination & Visual Tracking Exercises for Better Reading, Writing & Focus https://amzn.to/31l8Wyg

Brain Training Phonics: A Whole Brain Approach to Learning Phonics https://amzn.to/2KPR8dW

12 Weeks to Superior Memory & Mental Clarity: The Ultimate Cognitive Enhancement Program https://amzn.to/2HcgW2F

Brain Training Sight Words Grades 1 - 3 https://amzn.to/2Zc1LwL

Ready to Scan! BIG BOOK: Beginners, Intermediate & Advanced Visual Scanning Exercises https://amzn.to/2KQPtEX

One Minute Memory Exercises: Over 100 Memory Exercises to Boost Working Memory Kindle Edition https://amzn.to/2Z7SplG

ONE MORE THING

If you enjoyed this book, please leave a review on Amazon. We really value your opinion and strive to serve you. If you have any problems or questions with the program please contact us at adhdreading@gmail.com. We strive to serve our families, schools and communities.

Made in the USA
Monee, IL
24 May 2023

34471468R00020